Sum Yung Fun...a fresh breath of stale air

By

KENT ABBETT

ISBN: 1-4033-9872-0 (e-book)
ISBN: 1-4033-9873-9 (Paperback)
ISBN: 1-4033-9874-7 (Dust Jacket)

This book is printed on acid free paper.

1stBooks - rev. 03/14/03

Gratuitous Mentions

I would like to take this opportunity to thank the people whom unconditionally believed in me throughout my endeavors...

and for those in this book, you will always suffer from your voluntary mindless participation in values less than becoming of human beings... you poor sad inferior pathetic little people...

<u>*WHAT'S INSIDE*</u>

To the reader, each chapter is represented by the season in time: winter, spring, summer, and fall, etc..
The end of each chapter is followed by a brief anthology of the poems.

...to whom is this dedicated?
Why me of course...you see, it's not easy being me.

THE WINTER OF CONTENT

THE FIRST "Hey"

The first day you came into my life
we exchanged a familiar "hey."
How special a hey on this first day
you, I like.

Right back at ya, "hey."
The hey on this day
forever not to go
away in my mind.

This "hey" is a comfortable hey.
Our souls have met before in flight
like two angels passing
through a heavens light.

Your eyes flutter and gleam
with a lover's sprinkle, your gracious
smile tells me you're of a dream
come give to my soul your tinkle.

This first meeting of our souls
is a special acquaintance
as a treasure chest full
of love and joy.

I LOVE THEE

Before I knew your last name
the bold prediction soon the day
of marriage will come our way
I feel an unsuspecting love, my
visions of us prematurely.

Marriage, marriage I
dreamed of my proposal to
you in a horse drawn carriage.
I charmed you with my
promise of marriage.

Neither of our hearts expected
to tumble to the love of we,
soon will come the day
should you never go away.

As these words and thoughts
came to me I shared the
revelation with thee, you knew
what I spoke of, responding equally.

NATURAL BEAUTY

The favor I asked of you
you obliged me true,
the door opened rapidly
my travel bags in hand.

Your natural beauty
took my breath away.
Your clothed presence plain
and simple you first smiled
with a beautiful dimple.

Oh how true what elders say
upon making an impression,
for me with you t'was to be
my first beautiful lesson.

Your natural beauty
blew me away.
Later we talked and
laughed the night away.

I asked your permission,
surprised and curious
was your beautiful face
later we grew very close.

I remember kindly
putting you at ease,
this was my aim
only to please.

BUT OF COURSE, THE FIRST COURSE

The offer of libations
was a sort of titilation.
In the back, fireplace and
recycled resting space
the smile on your face.

The chit-chat was
enlightening and right.
Time passed like life
through out the night.

The text was simple
the text was light,
our reward for mind
swapping was end of night.

The quest of your lips
my hands hugging your hips.
You liked the affection of
my kiss, for you instant bliss.

The two of us soared to John st.
earlier the tempo set,
the feel of your soft skin
allowed me not to fret.

7

Kent Abbett

The moment of bonding
bodies had come
the assurance of safety
from now to kingdom come.

These words put you at ease
my love to you, aims to please.
Come, come sum yung fun
the magic of us was done.
It wasn't spike, but mutual like.

REST YOUR HEAD

I remember when this first occured,
you're such a sleeping beauty.
Your beautiful silky long black
hair I stroke on your head.

I wish for the rest of my life
rest your head softly in my bed.
Staring at you suspended eager
for the symbolism as we wed.

For the down and polyester
filler or natural feather,
you neither waver nor
change because of bad weather.

Come rest come rest your
beautiful gentle head,
I will protect you and love
you as you rest in my bed.

KNOWING

Getting to know you is
letting you know me.
Idiosyncratic likes and dislikes,
rollerblading, swimming or bikes.

Penmenship, light fuzz
on your upper lip,
might you be conservative, liberal,
bookworm, student, geek or hip.

Does your dexterity openly
show me your absolute clarity.
Do you consume vegetables
as your meal first or last,
late night delivery when it's past.

What really matters about learning
of one another is the willingness,
are we to be yearning for the
learning of a new love.

1 A. History of WINTER

We were first introduced at a restaurant. November 2000. We both worked there. This was her first night. She was training as a hostess. I sauntered through the front door running late as usual. I approached the hostess stand and noticed a new face.

We were introduced by a third party. She spoke first, after the introduction and said, "hey." She was very pretty. She had big beautiful eyes of a dark brown shade. Her smile gleamed so bright and sincere. I felt the soul of this person I had perhaps met before in the past.

I responded with an extended hand and a sexy, "hey." She was tickled pink by the touch of our hands and my direct sight line, deep into her eyes. She giggled girlishly and continued her duties.

I noticed as I walked away she was still checking me out. There seemed to be, in some spiritual manner, a human connection. We both felt it.

One evening after work a group of workers from the restaurant went to a club to have cocktails. She and I were part of this group. She and I had been working together for a couple of weeks and clicked, thus becoming fast friends. We discovered we had a lot of the same interests.

She engaged me in wonderful conversation and I reciprocated. The two of us had great ease in talking with one another. While having cocktails we laughed and discussed a wide range of topics. We discussed personal backgrounds and found out we had an amazing amount of similarities in our lives.

The evening started to wind down and some of the group dispersed. I asked her if she desired a cab home. I told her I would walk her out and hail the cab for her. As we exited I opened the building door and let her pass.

While hailing a cab I cracked wise with her and she broke out in laughter. I had a moment of spiritual enlightenment and boldly told her we would marry one day. She paused for a moment to let my statement sink in. She smiled and said, "I know."

I was heading to Florida for a couple of days to celebrate Christmas with my family, but because of my last minute booking I ended up reserving a flight at 6 a.m.. My plan was to work the night before and stay somewhere closer to the airport than where I lived. She and I discussed my dilemma and subsequently she offered to me her place to spend the night. I accepted.

The plan was to drop my luggage at her place before I went to work. After work she and I would go out to have drinks. When I arrived at her apartment that afternoon she opened the door donned in her bathrobe and no makeup. She was so beautiful. The thought struck me she was exposing herself without being self-conscious. This didn't seem to bother her. I was blown away by her natural beauty and friendliness.

I dropped off my luggage and we talked for a short period of time. She was very cool. She whizzed around her apartment doing things as we talked. She made me feel comfortable. I made her feel comfortable with the fact almost a complete stranger was going to stay at her place.

We established a certain trust at that point. All along while buzzing about, pausing at intervals to talk with me, she was flirtatious in her own way. It was cute and I kept thinking she really is very beautiful.

After work we whisked ourselves to her place so she could change. We laughed and had a drink. We jumped into a cab and I directed the cab driver to a place I thought would be perfect to have cool conversation with a very cool person.

When we arrived at my place of choosing she loved the little place. I escorted the two of us to the back of the lounge where it felt cozy and laidback. There was a fireplace, old couches that looked like they had been purchased from the Salvation army, huge paintings on the walls, and long drapes garnishing the walls. The ambiance was perfect.

We sat and had several cocktails. During our consumption of libations the topics of conversation were broad and intellectual. The stimulation of conversation was very tingley and playful. We joked and made fun of each other and made a great time of each others company.

Then in one bold moment I asked her if I could kiss her. She paused with a little girls twinkle in her eye and said yes. That first kiss melted the two of us. I wrapped my hands around her waist and thought we were going to make love right then and there. We made out on that couch for half an hour.

Then I suggested we go. We both knew from that point on what was going to happen. We jumped in a cab and went back to her place all the while continuing our saliva ceremony. We arrived at her place and immediately continued necking. We made our way to her bed, still fully clothed, and I laid her down. I began to undress her and she undressed me. Once fully naked we couldn't stop ourselves because of the sexy atmosphere we allowed ourselves to be in.

I could feel the nervousness in her body so I caressed her carefully to relax her and said, "it's okay, I'm not going to hurt you. I'm just going to make love to you." She immediately went limp like a noodle. She gave me her trust and I did not let her down. We made love for three hours. We couldn't get enough of each other.

13

We had been seeing each other for a month or so. The romance was hot and heavy. We made so much love she at times would push me away because I took her breath away and she took mine. We slept mostly at my place because she had a roommate and there was no privacy.

One night after our torrid love making we had pillow talk. I stroked her soft silky skin and her beautiful long silky hair. I confessed to her how much I liked being with her and our arrangement was very comfortable. She agreed. Then I proposed the idea to her we only see each other, be a couple or in quotation, "would you like to go steady?"

She laughed at my choice of words and repeated back to me the ideal of being monogamus. We laughed hugged conceded and then made more passionate love. Our rampant love making sessions would go on for hours at a time, normally three to four hours every night with multiple orgasms time after time. We stole each others breath away.

I told her I liked having her in my bed, fulltime. She stated how comfortable she felt in my presence and that she felt so safe in my arms and in general when we were together that nothing could happen to her while she was with me.

We started to fall in love and we didn't realize it at this point. It was all good.

Every moment we had was spent together. We went here, we went there. We went everywhere. I introduced her to my frequented social spots and she introduced me to her hangouts. We were both very open to the discovery stage of being with a new found love. We enjoyed each other's company immensely.

After our long love making sessions we would spend hours just caressing one another and staring into each others eyes. Normally these deep gazes would lead to more intense love making for hours.

Once we started to settle in with each others presence we delved into one anothers being. Noticing and paying attention to the small things about one another, the kinds of foods appealing to one another, left handed or right handed. The observation of one another grew to a point of constant inquiries, but not minding one bit what the other wanted to know. Our individual nuances were being nurtured by the other person. Neither one of us minded the scrutiny and we comfortably participated because we were falling in love with one another.

SPRING

YDA

On any given day be
it a dismal wintery day
or even on a glorious spring day
I'll love you anyway with YDA.

Anyday even with YDA.
YDA you can even show
to me on your off day,
I'll always love you this way.

What great phrases and words
can I bestow upon you this day,
whether you laugh or not I'll still
love you throughout the day.

Dopey, skippy, puss–puss, hey!
Bet you never heard of
anything quite so risque,
the world of YDA.

Oh, it's so cute we should
put it under a keyed lock,
as in Morocco like I explained
a running river and wash with a rock.

Kent Abbett

All the words in a day
keeping you laughing this way
I love you yes, yes,
on any given day, YDA.

THE DOVE

While we were making love
your beauty was that of a dove.
Gentle precious elegant love
as I looked at you from above.

The softness of your contours
only adds to the allures.
My soft gentle young dove,
deep inside to glide
like being on a slide.

You coo, ooh baby I love you,
reciprocal coo and you too.
I love your passionate coo too
ooh, ooh I love you too, with you
ooh, ooh make me coo too.

The soft gentle nature of a dove
I witness from above.
This is to me what
you're like my love.

YOUR POETRY

You are poetry in motion
the charm, the swagger when you walk,
the beauty of your face
and words when you talk.

Whenever I stare at you I can't
actually believe I'm with you.
When we make love my ears
are filled with the music of
your passionate utterances.

The supple lines of your
body are poetic by nature,
your touch makes magic
oh stare, oh stare.

The sheen of your beautiful hair
your face is that of an angels.
Tap, tap on your collarbone
I'm so lucky I'm not alone.

You are poetry in motion
whether you are idle or
mobile, still you are like
the gentle movement of the ocean.

SWEET & TART

Is your heart sweet
or is it tart?
You make sweet
with my heart,
you can make
me fall apart.

I hope I don't make tart
your beautiful little heart.
I'd like to think I make sweet
of a heart for you from
a different light.

Mm goy si, mm goy si
another plate arrives.
Oodles of delicious rice noodles
you are to me a canoodle.

Chopsticks, lip licks
are you happy?
It's sweet and tart, 2
rapidly beating hearts.
Are you filled up yet?

KEYS PLEASE

Fun fun where's the sun.
Seeking Larry, seeking Scotty,
seeking Ted Ted coconut head,
here comes the sun.

Stop stop, oh it's hot.
There's the blue water
on the side the whole thing,
let's make a quick drop.

The heat the heat
makes our hearts beat.
Being with you makes
me the most complete.

Is the pier that way?
At-ta-ta-ta-ta-ta
no problem man, the stress
will let us figure out the mess.

Look baby we have our
new word for the day,
the poor guy why did this
happen while we're so high.

Dive here dive there,
the importance of being

first in the water makes
this dive far from falter.

Bunnies bunnies our love
makes us like island bunnies.
I asked, you accepted
without pause or hesitation.

Fish fish not with a stick
we like ours with shells,
fins and gold of Mel's
fresh spilling over the side
of the eatery dish.

Fresh the fresh Meyers
dark with a spike of real
coconut makes your hung
the next a quagmire.

Little did we know we were
both 2nd generation best.
During this we fell in love
now forget the rest.

Bunnies of island fun
enjoying the lovers nest
soaking up the warm globals
you're 2nd generation best.

LARRY, LARRY

So limp in the grass back and
forth as you sway sway sway.
I found you rescued you
and preserved you anyway.

You're good and dead but you
probably drank with Hemingway
on what was for both
of you a better day.

Seen from the top
you looked like
an old but small
discarded mop.

I knew I knew about your
old spanish armour the talk
that once a year you and
yours would make the walk.

Spangled and tangled
I dropped to scoop your chin,
gave the signal to the top
hide and slide, stuff you in a fin.

Now you're home with me
ready to varnish and put
the base on a base with
the date and word KEY.

TOUCHING THERE

Nothing should come between
us my sweet young love
not even the dreaded
over emphasized latex glove.

The softess caress there
frequently now reminds me
of the first time, sending
electricity through my spinal hair.

Like the conductor of an
orchestra making history
we indulged ourselves
in each others mystery.

Upon instruction of coupled hands,
you're amazed by grasps and groans.
It's much sexier with another
rather than going it alone.

Whether swinging or swaying
quarter notes, half notes or
full notes this is uniquely
our music when we're playing.

SPIKED YOUR HEART

To the best of one's recollection
t'was a warm spring day,
elegance in the blowing wind
maybe sometime in May.

A striking blow of white
near, yet from behind.
Quizzical turn of the head
your eyes, love was said.

Love in your eyes the look
of something gone wrong
like a sledge hammer as the
sound of Liberty went DONG.

Please, please don't be mad
my dear young love understand
with all encompassing, to you I
give all that my bilging heart had.

Yes yes am I to blame?
I love you just the same.
Your heart, you were right
whom has spiked your heart,
hence the sudden blow of white.

29

I spiked your heart
my young love, to you
I explain truly my sweet
the love I give is like art.

Fine yes fine this art
give it enough time I
don't mind the blame, but
together we spiked your heart.

ANIMALS

They exist so deeply within
you were so passionately introduced
to many dormant sleeping pets
located very near the tan-tien.

There's one for this
and one for that.
There's one for daytime
and one for the midnight.

There's one for every
imaginable occasion
if you are willing to let
the beast into the maison.

Over and over you love mine
and passionately I love yours.
When ensconced in the throws
of passion you open the doors.

Signs located 'round the zoo,
"Don't feed the animals"
have yet to offer to humans
the deepest of simple clues.

I fed yours and you mine.
My love you know which animal
of mine is true, both of us intertwined.
Feed the animal, need the animal.

THE HEAT OF YOUR NIGHT

Out of nowhere deep into
the night all of a sudden
the heat from within you
came to the surface like an oven.

I blanketed you like a skin
to take away your heat
of that scary moment though
you were rapidly diminishing.

The thought, my thought
of what fast action I should do,
I summonsing Dr. Feelgood.
I'll explain him to you.

He's a very helpful dude
to the troubled person
he can help and exude,
Dr. Feelgood is on call.

Medicinally Dr. Feelgood
can change your mood.
Trust me relax and enjoy,
this may not be conventional
but still I am your toy.

I'm checking your heart,
your pulse your rhythm
my methods are sound how
can we ever be apart.

Budump, budump goes the heart
I think I've transformed you
now you can understand, just
enjoy my feel good art.

Now that you're better
a little sweat and some flutter
you were feeling ill
accounts receivable
you will get the bill.

He recommends love
instead of consuming pills,
piggyback ride now I'll
take you up the hill.

We kiss and laugh
oh Dr. Feelgood
you've definitely
mastered your craft.

Within moments of treatment
that he prescribes to the ailing,

your extreme heat went and
you were no longer flailing.

Dr. Feelgood where were you
educated in this method of mood,
all that can be said is this
is one sure fire cool dude.

<u>SLIPPING INTO OBLIVION</u>

Oh god how I care for you
the worst thing would be
this feeling of losing you,
I think I'm losing you.

Why, why, God help from
the sky I can't handle this
or maintain this current
cycle of loss and abyss.

You're the only one I'd
never be able to hurt.
Oh forgive me my love,
bless me from above
engulfing her like a glove.

Have I been non-angelic
less than an example of perfect.
The debt has been repayed don't
double-up collection of debt.

Not this way, I say
I'll eat all the vegetables
promise, just I can't pay
for my wrongs this way.

The result of my current monotony
I perceive to be this circumstance
in life, although I informed you
of my strife before and ask
you to wait for my romance.

Two sevens pass, alas.
I regain momentum
through lunchtime liasions
of sweat, moisture and sex eyes,
finally the circumstance will pass.

2 A. History of SPRING

We had been seeing each other for a few months. We were not selfconscious of ourselves around each other. Characteristics of our individual personalities would be displayed through behavior and language. Usually certain faces or thought up words were presented to the other. Words and pet names or insider descriptives were always good for humors sake in conversation. We were being silly in love.

I have always had an arsenal of bizarre sayings. I introduced her to one by the name of "yda." The abbreviation stands for "your dirty ass." There was a story I read about a tribe that bathed in a river and used rocks and stones for scrubbing devices. Just a term to describe people of low personal hygiene.

Regardless of the specific words, usually what ever came to my imagination was funny and it would make her laugh. This is what our romance had blossomed into. Fun, love, and laughter. Many of the "words" we discovered to be funny, also turned into sexy language for us to communicate through.

She was beautifully contoured. Long lean limbs, beautiful graceful lines. Once while making wild passionate love I viewed these lines with great admiration. So elegant so precise. Even her sexy utterances were becoming extremely intoxicating.

During one of our marathon love sessions the "love" word creeped out. This particular affection initially was puzzling to her, but at that very moment the relationship took off in a new direction. The soft passionate sounds of making love grew deeper and more passionate than ever before. Deep feelings were surfacing.

The love developing between the two of us was ever present because of the "love" word being frequently used. When she and I were in public or alone the sound of the love bird was always humming.

We were together all the time or at least it seemed like it. We were intoxicated by each others presence be it at work or at play. The deep scrutiny of each others smallest habits were so cute to us. Some humans are amazingly beautiful to watch.

I started to appreciate the fine side of her. Shapes of her fingers, shapes of her toes. The wave of her hand. The way she crossed her legs. The silky soft inflections of her voice. Her walk, as I told her, was truly a swagger. Not like a man, but cocky. For a girl it was "tomboyish" in a sexy way.

When she would come out of the shower I would become thristy watching her dry off or towel dry her hair. Watching her dress was such a beautiful sight because of the fluidity she sustained while in motion. Ebb and flow.

The finer cuisines were becoming an important part of our time spent together. We went out often to experience different restaurants. Eating a fine meal with a sexy woman is sexy in itself. We both loved eating, but especially after making love whether it was morning, afternoon, or night.

She once introduced me to a better quality Chinese restaurant. Neither one of us had been there before. Upon our arrival we went to the top floor. Most other patrons didn't realize they could go to the top floor. Instantly we flipped over the experience of consuming this restaurants cuisine.

She taught me a chinese phrase once. Thanking one for the food when brought to the table. I couldn't stop saying thank you in between the many courses of food they kept bringing to the table. My appetite was of monstrous proportions after our marathon love sessions. We kept raving over the texture and quality of the delicasies. We were both happy when eating at this place.

We would transcend when eating regularly at this delicious intoxicating establishment. We had become regulars. We would enter with sex eyes and empty stomachs. Our hearts were beating so fast from eating so much and being so connected to one another that we were getting lost in each others world.

I was planning my vacation for early March and wanted to go some place warm with clear blue skies, bright sun, tasty beaches. One day while she and I were working together I brought up the topic of where to go. Her opinon was relevant.

I asked her if she had ever been to the Florida Keys before. She had not. I asked her, without hesitation, if she would like to go with me. We were that close in a short period of time. Traveling for couples is a good test to determine the patience and caring of the relationship. She accepted without hesitation. I guaranteed her safety. She gave me trust.

The tempo of the trip was first set by renting a convertible to drive from the airport to the Keys. I promised her I would set the precedent for fun and sun. I taught her about the importance of getting back to nature which first meant making love in the car. We would stop where the ocean and highways meet to take an impromptu swim.

We ate fresh seafood everyday. We drank Pina Colada's by the gallon and we made wild romantic animalistic love in the sun.We snorkeled near ancient islands. We saw gold from ancient wrecks and gave names to our vehicles and other goofballs we encountered.

I showed her what it meant to be one with the ocean and earth as she discovered when we saw a nurse shark in the water. I promised her no harm would come to her, but she needed to stay close to me. The ensuing lust that vacationed with us was at a new level. We grew so close during this trip and fell in love with one another. Lovers libido fueled by warm romantic carribean flavors.

Laying on a dock 90 miles from Cuba I noticed an object in the water. The next time I went into the water I investigated the object to figure out what it was. As I approached the object it had perfect synchronicity with the current of the ocean, mildly active.

The closer I came to the object my senses heightened. I knew it was a lobster. She and I gave him the name of "Larry." Larry was laying in the grass moving back and forth. He was tiny, but still he was a lobster. Initially I dove on him to observe. The second dive I snatched him from the clutches of the ocean and the grass.

Larry was dead. His shell was perfectly in tact. Not one blemish. Although the meat of this crustacean was nonexistent. The reason being small fish gobbled him up. Larry was approximately 12" in length.

I scooped him up swam back to the dock and carefully smuggled him out of the Florida Keys. Because the Florida Keys are a National Preserve my action could have landed me in jail with stiff financial penalties.

I scored this souvenir for her. I explained to her the risk I took and the reason behind it. To perfectly preserve a small creature and mount it. This souvenir was far beyond any photograph or tee-shirt I could present to her, but she didn't understand the value of such a find.

I told her the history behind Larry. Once a year there is a migration of Spanish Key Lobsters from the east coast of Florida to the Bahamas. This migration is known as the "Lobster crawl." Thousands upon thousands of Lobster in single file trek hundreds of miles to spawning grounds in the Bahamas.

She and I loved the physical discoveries of our bodies, together. Couples whom are not afraid to experience and experiment with sex ultimately become physically addicted to one another. Our sex fests had only increased in the months since we were together.

Kent Abbett

We masturbated each other while making love or engaged in some sort of self pleasure together more and more. We experimented with different positions, different locations whether indoors or in public places. We knew what got each other off and how to perfectly please one another. She couldn't get enough of my sex nor could I get enough of hers.

One beautiful spring day early in the afternoon she and I were getting dressed, again, to enjoy a lunch outing. We both had the day off so we decided to make a day of the outing. We had made fabulous love all morning and we were famished.

I was fixing my hair at her dresser bureau and after cracking something wise to her she wacked me with a pair of her slacks. She didn't hurt me. When I turned around to voice my shock of her reaction I saw something in her eyes that spoke volumes.

She had fallen in love with me! Her eyes said it all. I knew it. We often had joked about me spiking her heart, rather than her cocktail, but that particular day she was saying to me, "I have fallen in love with you."

My charm was the only reason as well as the love I gave her. I told her of the nonverbal communication in her eyes and she laughed knowing I was right. Essentially we made the other fall in love and it was perfect! We were so in love with one another floating on cloud nine, instead of eating we made love again and ordered our food in.

I had an extremely high appetite for great sex, not just any sex, but rather great sex. My appetite had finally found someone that truly enjoyed making love as much as I did. The fact we were deeply in love with one another only fueled our desire for one another.

I explained to her I had an animal for every occasion. The animals needed to be fed when they woke up. Of course not all of the animals were awake at the same time. While one was awake the others were dormant, until they woke to stimulation craving satisfaction.

We discovered she had some animals that needed feeding too. She knew this and relied on me to feed her appetite for sex, love, food, partying, nuturing, and intellect. We fed each others animal constantly.

One night we were settling down to bed and I mentioned to her how hot she was. She acknowledged this by indicating she felt weak. Almost as though she was becoming sick with a fever. I fed her some aspirin to bring her temperature down.

After 30 minutes her temperature had not moved as she was burning up. Because her blood was boiling she became very horny and I advised her how I could help her to bring the temperature back to normal. She thought my suggestion to be strange, but she allowed me to apply my medicinal training to her.

We made mad passionate love for a couple of hours. Tossing and turning in the bed. Sweating, moaning and groaning she pushed me away from her silky body. She proclaimed her temperature had gone down to her amazement.

I concurred through feeling her forehead. She was as cool as the other side of the pillow. I learned this trick many years previous and she wanted to know how I learned this. I told her it was my secret, but when she felt better I would send her a bill for my services rendered. When she felt sick again she knew she could count on me to make her pain feel better within a romantic period of time.

My work would demand most of my time over the next two weeks and I explained this to her. I emphasized to her we were not breaking up nor was I losing interest in her. A small period required most of my attention. I made her feel comfortable about this. Or so I thought.

Half way through my endeavor we hadn't seen much of each other and I felt we were drifting apart by accident. I had a sick feeling about growing apart. I tried to hedge my bet by explaining this in advance, but she could only see that I wasn't giving her enough attention. People mentally weak are like this.

I felt bad about her not having my full attention, but I am not a needy person as she was showing me she was. I pleaded with her to be patient.

This period of time would pass by then we would carry on as we had in the past. Mad passionate love making every day.

She was going out with people, friends or not I don't know, every night. I sensed she was bored with my current situation and she was looking for attention elsewhere. This was a dangerous equation for her because she was a social butterfly and a raving beauty.

I was losing her and I felt it. After the couple of weeks were finished I thanked her for her understanding and we started having lunchtime liasions every day for about three weeks. Sex, sex, & more sex. I promised her I would make up for the lost time. And I did. We fell back in love with one another again.

I didn't know what she had been up to in that period of time, I would later find out during the summer. Her blunderheaded mistake would show to me her insecurities, infidelities, and her childish like mind and what she was like in dealing with her. She was a victim of her own selfishness.

SUMMER

WAKING

Better to wake in yours
or to wake in mine.
Matter does not, what does
us putting in the time.

The nape of your long neck
the fuzz of your lower back.
You're so warm my heart flutters
I caress you as I kiss your face.

You are so beautiful my love
I can't help myself watching
you in sleep state you
are my sleeping beauty.

Wake my love wake,
so that we may engage
in the moistures of your lake
only if you are to wake.

Grunts and groans,
aches and moans.
Are you awake my
sweet young love?
Oh wake dear love wake.

LINGUINI ARMS

When I wrap my arms
around you from behind
you sense and feel deep
down that I am kind.

Not even between us
must a word be said,
love, tenderness and romance
swirls within our heads.

My imagination wanders
as you're tightly gathered
within my arms.
Is this gentle warmth
of our compassionate minds?

Caring, two hearts, beat as one
my hands softly caress your tummy,
imagine our romantic passions
could make you a future mommy.

I love you my dear
so true am I to you
always I'm gentle when
your presence is near.

47

You wrapped in my
oily linguini arms,
we teter and rock like
that of our slow song,
never will I bring YOU harm.

ODE TO YOUR EYES

I see you from here
see you from there,
while you work I spy cop
a peek from everywhere.

When you see me, I the spy,
you giggle and smile passers-
by think you're strange
only we know the difference
our rampant love range.

I love you in frills, I love you in lace
when our eyes at a distance lock
I love you for that smile blossoming
upon your beautiful face.

By the river that night
I dared you to kiss me
under the light
oh how you make my liver quiver.

You passed most of the test
so you dated some of the rest
oh my dear precious what do you
think now that you've had the best.

49

Kent Abbett

Put gently your head to rest
on my bare naked chest
I hope you'll always love
and be with the best.

MY BLOOD STIRS

The blood boils and toils
my blood can no longer
contain, harness, manage
or deal with bubbling boil.

When you pass me by
we give each other the wink of an eye.
Yes this has become a spoil
and I explain this to you
how you make my blood boil.

The fantasy thought of us
intertwined and tightly taut
like that of an old rummy sailors
carefully constructed knot.

Why do you make me
feel this uncontrollable way?
I'm excited, confused and perplexed
by your romantic stay.

With you the romance I
dedicated becomes a toil
you reciprocated through spoil.
Oh my sweet dear love how you
make my blood stir and boil.

SPLOTTY-DOTTY

Splotty-dotty, splotty-dotty, splotty-dotty
splotty-dotty, splotty-dotty, splotty-dotty
splotty-dotty, splotty-dotty, splotty-dotty
splotty-dotty, splotty-dotty, splotty-dotty

<u>THE SCUM OF OTHERS</u>

Oh they tried, they tried
we rejected the proposed
wedge between us.
Deeper and deeper goes the wedge.

But wait, strength and growth
becomes our best defense.
Like two cachimono's don't
go away mad or jealous, you're
out of your caliber, just go away.

They're disgusting, cheesy,
low clase and garbage anyway.
Oh no you evil zions by
MY rules we'll have to play.

My game is level A.
Don't try ambulance chaser
and island jezebel because the kid
will blow your minds away.

She and me are tighter
smarter and more of a team
you have no choice but
to take the loosers walk.

53

The two true lovers win, they stay.
Try the perilous weak they may,
but oh strong love of mine
together forever we'll stay.

HIGH

The sky so blue by day
and charcol by night,
how high will you
make your rocket fly.

Condoning is my sorrow
I'll forever reserve my
condemnation for the
remaining tomorrow.

I beg for your forgiveness
for my lack of direction,
in the always liberal
and hectic situations.

Should've, could've, would've
I beg for your forgiveness the
pot calling the kettle black,
in order to go back my responsibility
in hindsight is to take up the slack.

The time you had an embarrassing
event for the two of us,
I was so enamoured of you
I was absolutely clueless.

55

I ask for your forgiveness my
allowing your rocket to fly so high,
when I watched from above
yes I did control the sky.

The basis for any great love
not letting the other get
out of control or letting
the other fly so high.

WHY DO WE FIGHT

It's healthy to air it out,
the waste of time what's it about.
Nothing. I care for you my passions
run so very deep it's true.

I'm blind, I'm weak, I'm
stubborn let's not do it this way.
I'm leaving you're in your robe
bless me and let her stop me.

Wake up dummy, she did.
Love her now, weep together
blame each other laugh
at the nonsense, hindsight.

Why do we fight
don't be stubborn,
don't be selfish
my job is to love you.

In the end oui see
the words and ideals
exchanged through a
time of loves suspension
matters not a bit.

Silly is always the result
of young lovers in love,
when all that counts is
reconciliation of two passioned hearts.

3 A. History of SUMMER

We had a small dilema, she and I. Where should our nights be spent together. Her roommate moved out and she spread her wings in her apartment. She loved the idea of having a place all to herself. She lived very close to our work place. I did not. For me the decision was simple, as long as I had her in my arms.

We grew together as a couple and equally grew closer and closer because we spent every free moment we had with one another. Our activities at night or during the day were together. Waking up in one anothers arms was becoming comfortably common place and we both loved it.

Sometimes we would stay at my place, but most times we stayed at her place because of the convenient location and we were efficient in quality time with each other. We were becoming one.

We both realized how special our romance had become as evident when going to sleep or waking up in each others arms. She dug every minute of our time together and so did I.

Our love for one another had reached such a pleasant pennacle for the two of us. We were in love with one another as freightening, apocalyptic, and absolute as it were, neither one of us fought our feelings. This meant were we so vulnerable to one another yet the trust we had built between each other was unprecedented to us that we had no insecure feelings whatsoever.

When we snuggled or embraced that moment was as real as true love gets. Freedom of insecure like of one another was the plateau we had reached. It was clear to the two of us when we looked into each others eyes or clasped hands. The touch of the senses was heightened and sharp.

We joked and rationalized about us being parents to children we would bring into this world. We agreed mutually our parenting skills would be wonderful. Only if the reality of marrying one another was as real as the tingling in our romantic hearts. We loved each other so terribly bad we had to make love every minute we were together like newlyweds. Oh yeah.

She had the most beautifully colored eyes I had ever seen on a woman or another human being for that sake. When we worked together I played hide and seek games with her. My objective was to see if she could tell when I was near to her. Was my loving energy enough to bring about her awareness of my proximity. Yes.

When I copped a peek at her and she knew I was watching her she acknowledged with smiling eyes and a sexy warm smile. On lookers had no idea the game we played, but we didn't care because all that mattered was our communication with one another.

I dared her one night to engage in a bizarre test of our coworkers awareness of us being together. We were down by the river. We walked over to a street light stood there and engaged in a long luscious kiss. This romantic gesture with a hint of danger thrilled her senses to no end. She thought me to be crazy, but I once again exemplified what trust meant and protection of loved ones.

She passed the dare with flying colors and was more than stimulated by the off-the-wall test. She believed me to be some sort of spiritual god that willed events to happen. Her perception was correct. I was and I did.

She and I engaged in many love making sessions at different times of the day. The self control of being in public together and not making love right on that spot was over whelming. She lived in me and I lived within her.

When we were working together I would pass her by and slightly brush up against her hand or arm. She would give me a look of "make love to me now." The excitement running wildly through our bodies was hard to contain. Every so often I would sneak her to a private corner and lay a huge sexy kiss on her and walk away before she could utter one word.

Equally she would think of ways to drive me crazy with her presence. Paging me or sending another person as a go between to summons me. Everytime we had work related business respectively we knew a touch of the other was inevitable. Our libido's were presenced and always available to the other. We had become great lovers…understatement!

The celebration of sound is an awe inspiring perk in life. The sounds of making love is the golden goose. She and I reached the point in our relationship when making love the others' moans and groans were symphonic music in our ears. Rhythmic in nature competing utterances are only part of the joy of making love.

Glistening bodies fiercly sweating while in the throws of anothers passionate soul creates skin music. Slipping and sliding and dull popping of two bodies squirming together have a definite and distinct sound. Gushing bodily fluids dripping vertically and horizontally across and in between two naked bodies provides a membrane varnish of passion and transendental echoes.

The celebration of sounds when making love.

I went ballistic in my own cool calculated diplomatic way. Suddenly I was listening to a coward, coke addict, drug dealer, alcoholic (did I forget to mention he was a lawyer, and not very good at that) s.o.b. at my place of work tell me he was screwing my girlfriend.

61

A mentally challenged troll told me he was seeing my girlfriend. I was thinking of describing my intial reaction as "surprised," but that would be too kind in telling about the nerve of some low clase subhumans. I sent the demented humpback diseased one away with a word of advice.

I confronted her for enlightenment wanting to seek truths. More importantly I wanted to know what the _ _ _ _ was going on. She was cornered and I gave her one chance to come clean. She told me *only* what I needed to know. Bad decision for her and a cheesey response.

Their one night stand, or so I was told it was only one night, from months ago came back to haunt her. I'm stuck in the middle of a situation that is getting out of control rapidly. This ghetto fabulous lawyer was trying to manipulate my relationship to his liking. I didn't like his decision nor the remark about giving my girl an std!!

The lie she told me was his basis for an ill-fated decision. After she freaked out about the situation and I read her the riot act I moved swiftly to quash the little ambulance chaser. He didn't know whom he was dealing with OR what I was capable of.

Her shock wore off days later, but as far as the initial day of ground breaking news to her, I should have cracked her in the mouth to get her attention. Things made no sense. Disinformation or fractionary information is simple to decipher...someone is telling b.s.. I raised the stakes to protest the game being run down on me. Other noses really got bent out of shape. What a shame!

Knowing how to deal with such scurvy and his date, the fake blond scurvy, I resolved the situation. My girl "dopey" made the situation a little more screwed up. With my guidance she and I rose above the ill- equipped children playing their little games.

The ground was shaky between my girlfriend and I for numerous reasons. She was moving away in a couple of months and planning to return a few months after that. We had been through an unbelieveable situation and I didn't trust her because I sensed she wanted to tell me something. I knew what it was. She probably had been a tramp with other men while we were lovers. How cheap it was. The drugs didn't help her and considering her health set backs she was being a fool.

She was partying out of control with drugs, alcohol and tricking people's minds. She felt cocky for no reason other than she had no self-esteem. I tried to build her back up and give a sense of pride to her, make her feel good about herself. I gave a lot of latitude to her antics and I also loved her. I made many exceptions for her.

My liberal approach to our love was too slack. She should have been on a leash so that she didn't cause trouble to herself or other individuals. She thought she was smart, but the dummies always do anyhow. She embarrassed me one evening at work when she got whacked on Martini's. She puked and stumbled all over the place like an idiot. The selfish ways of a child was catching up to the young adult.

I wondered the next day how could I love her when she wasn't showing guilt or remorse for the escapade from the night before. She complained about her hangover. I could have been fired from work because of her antics. But I didn't think she needed a lecture because she professed her maturity and intelligence. My instincts were pure and clean, but my heart and head were soiled by love.

We were airing out some frustration between the two of us. Mostly because of her behavior and stupid mistakes we would have the silliest arguments. Verbal altercations always ending in making love, but nevertheless childest situations because of her crappy judgement.

Still I didn't trust her and she wore a thin acrylic veil of deception. I confronted her one night after she slipped up in making a remark about something. I dressed while shouting at her and all the while she sat on the bed denying and lieing about the scandal with the customer. She had such a look of desperation on her face. She just wanted to scream out her confession and cleanse her soul, but she had no sense of bravery.

Like children whom don't understand about truths being less painful than lies, she cried as she chased me down to the street in her lingerie. Still she didn't have the intestinal fortitude to just say the truth. I cut her some slack. We made wild love for the rest of the night. I loved this girl in such a way as to compromise my own morals, integrity, common sense.

I should have dumped her there on the sidewalk as she was scantly dressed that evening. I didn't think she was capable of evil doings, or better yet I didn't want to believe she was cold and calculating.

FALL

Kent Abbett

WHY DID YOU GO AWAY

The tears in your eyes
say all you need to say
this hot Queens morning,
tell me you want to stay.

I will forever treasure the night
just past watching you buzz
about packing and stacking
and freaking out what to do
with trivial possessions.

We snuggle under the covers
while making love and the
cool summers breeze blow
in through the open windows.

Entwined are our moist
bodies for this summer day,
passion and love forever
concisely, stay with me this way.

When finally you rest
your head on my chest
our emotions rush to the
surface and your delicate
tears dribble down your face.

We exchange pleasantries
and fantasy ideas for the
future but all along you
knew the emptiness of your
words were the conclusion.

We promise each other to
try the distance romance,
not knowing of one another
would we actually sustain the stance.

The rumble of jets make
my heart pound more,
please I don't want it this way,
to be by myself won't you
reconsider and stay.

I miss you I miss you
I close my eyes in the hallway
and caress your face, the eyes,
the lips, the cheeks to never
forget the feeling of your face.

The reality as you go away
I might never see you again,
so I trace your mouth and chin
and feel this might be the last stay.

We'll call, write and e-mail too,
can you promise me in the
far off land of your exploits
that'll you be honest and true.

We'll try, we'll try
but ultimately through
time having to cry,
oh why did you ever fly.

STRONG BELIEF

The trick my love is
to sustain and stay strong
because before you realize it
rendezvous will be our song.

Believe in me you'll see,
you prompt don't give up,
look I weep like a pup
soon you'll learn from me
not to cave in or give up.

With all my words of hype
never in my young 40 years
have I engaged love or
conversation with a
person of your type.

I encouraged you but my
love you wouldn't stay,
so for now we're apart
will it stay this way.

<u>DAY OF INFAMY</u>

Ring ring what's that
confounded sounding thing.
A call so early for me,
9 a.m. vision still blurry.

Your voice to me was
concerned and frightened,
2 magnificent twins devastated
and no longer vertically heightened.

My words only of gratefulness
of your current absence hence
I love you, I love you was
the main thrust of sentence.

Oh no oh no don't
know where to go.
I love you, I love you
so glad you don't live at zero.

In the weeks previous
before you left, that
evening to you I showed
the location of future horror,
gratefulness of your move I owed.

71

COMMS IN TIME

The conversations only
build my pulsations
when the chime of your voice
wriggles in my mind.

The subject or the content
of our conversations has
always been truly an
intellectual engagement.

Long gone for now are
the iris to iris situations,
via Graham Bell I love
to hear your whispers.

As I hear the sounds I glisten
I only wish you were in my
presence to witness my
excitement as I listen.

Childhood dreams, business
schemes, world affairs, weather
or parental disputes I'll
listen and listen and listen.

We've been voyeurs and perhaps
naughty in recent conversation,
all in all with you our passions
build to overwhelming sexy pulsations.

Whilst I imagine your face
the many miles between us
give you the much needed
and emphasized space.

Time time the pendulum
strikes infinite times.
The absurdity of quality events
we can't spend in time
punishes me like a capital crime.

ITINERARY

The countdown has begun
until we meet and continue
our much awaited hugs,
laughter and lovers fun.

The billet has been purchased
as we strategized exactly when,
but no so much where because
my love you relocated there.

The twelfth minus one
my love will be the time,
but yet the clock hands don't
move quite like our chime.

Crawling it does my desires
sprawling across many oceans
and mountains to reach you
to feel the magic again.

We've established many events
for entertainment, but the most
important is that of us locked
arm in arm against hearts harm.

Each time of speaking we
concur the pendulum swings,
but not rapidly as wished
in our private dreams.

Patience is virtuous my
young love I'll be delivered
from above ascending for
an entire moons life process
only to be descending in one less.

Soon soon my beautiful
flower when the special hour
has brushed us together
what will be our power.

4 A. History of FALL

We were awakened by a phone call. We overslept. She was late for her flight to Hong Kong and the car service was waiting downstairs. No time to make love again. We drag her big bags downstairs and loaded them in to the car. The driver whisked us off to the airport.

She spent all but 4 hours the day before packing for her move back to H.K.. Of the 4 hours, 2 were spent sleeping and 2 were spent making love to me until we saw each other a few months from then. That was the plan. We were going to take a sincere stab at keeping our love alive from half way around the world from one another.

We loved each other so much despite the problems from a couple of months previous. We reconciled and carried on with a terrific romance.

I kept wondering though if she would be honest and faithful while we were apart, temporarily.

She had a debacle at the ticket counter with overweight luggage. While transferring some of her possessions to a box her panties she had packed fell and spew all over the ground. Her intimacy displayed to complete strangers. I flew into action and saved her the embarrassment. The stress on the two of us was immense.

At the last security checkpoint we hugged for 20 minutes. She cried. I stayed strong for the two of us. At least I thought her tears were for us, but really they were for me not out of sadness, but rather for pity. That's so sad.

We spoke everyday after she arrived in H.K.. As a matter of fact we spoke a couple of times each day and we e-mailed each other constantly.

This is how the beginning begins. It's all peaches and cream not to mention expensive in the beginning. I felt it was the beginning of total uncertainty for us in the future.

I explained to her about my previous long distance romances. None of which were successful. The theorem is to stay strong and be positive about future travel to see one another. She said she understood and it wouldn't be a problem. I never thought there to be a problem with it.

We discussed her new surroundings and her old discoveries. She described to me on the phone what her new home was like and how excited she was being back home. She had a lot of work to do in a short time before she was to return to the U.S..

We had the most delightful conversations I had ever experienced with another human being. We got sexy with each other on the phone and relived the beautiful moments we had spent together for the past 10 months. We laughed, we cried. We fed off each others strengths and energy. We spoke of the first embrace we would have the next time we saw each other.

I will never forget this day for the rest of my life. My beautiful country, my beautiful city, my beautiful patriotism. I walked through the WTC's for the last time after work at 2 a.m. to catch my subway home on September 11, 2001.

When I woke later that morning I woke to horror. She called me from H.K. to see if I was at work. Of course I wasn't because I work at nights. But why did she call me so early. The tremble in her voice alarmed me. She was stuttering and babbling about the World Trade Centers and my t.v..

The only thing I could say to her when I realized the WTC's were viciously attacked by terrorists, like the schyster lawyer, was how glad I was she moved away. As terrible as it sounds my gratefulness was unprecedented. I made sure she understood what I was saying by reminding her of the "deja vu'."

Just 10 days or so earlier on our last date we were walking by the WTC's. She lived 1 1/2 blocks east of ground zero and 1 block north of Wall st.. I reminded her of the terrorists alert we had been on all summer long. She gave me a look of utter confusion. Yeah, I showed where she lived in relation to WTC's, Wall st., and the Federal Reserve.

My life was changed forever from that day forward...

She and I were on a regular telephone schedule and e-mail schedule. By now the pain of her leaving had smoothed out and we found ways to carry on as though we were still in the same city, although she was on the other side of the world.

I couldn't wait to hear her voice on the phone when she called. The sound of her voice made me trip down memory lane. I missed having her in my arms so much. She concurred. We both agreed what a special relationship we had and we should nurture it as much as possible.

We talked about how wonderful it was making love to one another. I introduce her to phone sex and she really enjoyed it. We engaged in voyeurism to the max. She told me I was naughty. She was right, but she didn't mind being naughty with me.

We discussed intimate family secrets like two really close people do. I gave her direction in dealing with family issues based on my personal experiences. One minor problem I wasn't raised in a dysfunctional family. I expressed my love for her and reassured her of the future between us would be fine, but she must listen to the voice of reason not bias advice from her family.

I sensed doubt in her voice sometimes when we talked. She had others telling her what to do and they supported their rational with material objects. She was being set-up for complete domination through monetary bribing. She was wavering and I knew the possibility of our future was hanging in the balance. Her elders were performing a psych job on her and she was beginning to cave in. Truly though I knew what she wanted to do and so I kept reminding her of that.

Finally she broke and told me 75 % truth of her scandal during the summer with the schyster lawyer. Even at that it wasn't the full truth. She presented herself to him like a tramp and so he treated her like a tramp. She couldn't understand why. Before she moved back there further contact between them took place. When asked about the lies she said, "I told you only what you needed to know." Pretty shallow!

Finally the plans were set in motion. We were going to rendezvous in H.K. in early winter. I was going to chase the girl of my dreams, so I believed she was, to the opposite side of my world. Even though I was pulling a rabbit out my hat by scraping and scrambling to finance this trip she finally worked with me on setting an itinerary.

I had traveled somewhat around the world, not extensively, but proud of my passport stamps. The longest flights I had been on were NY to Paris. I told her of this and she coached me how to deal with the 24 hour flight. Two suns and one moon.

I felt in my heart this trip was going to be the most exciting event in my life. She agreed. The time we were going to spend together sent chills up and down her fragile little spin. She told me, "you just made me wet."

I promised her I would do more than that when I finally had her in my clutches.

79

Kent Abbett

Our planning the trip together, she on her end and me on mine, showed us how good a test this would be for the relationship because we had been apart for a couple of months. Absence makes the heart grow fonder. This trip was about the two of us. Just the two of us.

<u>WINTER, AGAIN</u>

STEAMING AHEAD

The time has come to move on
with parcels in hand although
the road has been rurally rough
hence the times past for me.

First my sweet love leaves
and I'm left to greave and you
find new surroundings not so
new but different than previous.

Two twins take an attack from
evil doers that blanket my fair
city with tears, anger, a nations
mourning and worldwide pity.

My life is the upside down
cake left in the oven for extra
crispness and sickness of
wonderful ingredients.

Ghetto girl was a sour twirl
to drop it like a bad habit,
resent my charity when her
time of desperation was meant.

All throughout the ying
without a yang we remedied
the pains with our love and
compassions soon to know
we'd be wrapped in passions.

Oh big bird deliver this
carcass safely and willingly
to the part of the world
where my love awaits me.

THE LIGHT OF FLIGHT

Touching down feeling ground
my mind is wobbly but the
thought of seeing finally
you fills my heart round.

Oh flight oh flight
I can finally see
the exotic light
of the traveled night.

The park becomes dark
don't let this trip be a lark.
I'm so anxious, so anxious
maybe I'll parachute down.

The lines of time wind
me around in a circle
of amazement. New people,
new faces only I seek one
in these foreign spaces.

Clearance for Clarence
finally releases my full
attention to getting out
to the love of my life.

THE FIRST NIGHT

Whisked away on a rail
my heart begins to sail
now that my side is filled
with your very sight.

Situated in a room with
a view that is less
than your presence and
warmth in my arms.

Rantings, raving of a new
finally we settle in to show
how much each of us care
with a gentle stroke
through the others hair.

Twisting, turning our long
awaited love is burning,
seems like not a moment
has been skipped, now
the reality of the trip.

So long I waited equally you
for the moments of passion
moving in our bodies through
and through yet now it's true.

My sweet love finally
we are together again,
watch out world the
love fest will now begin.

HONG KONG LIGHTS

Twas said by you
the vision is for you,
the sights of the nights
are mysteriously true.

Venture here venture there
together we will discover
this beautiful city floating in air,
naturally hand in hand is fare.

Lan Kwai Fong until dawn
Thai Thai makes me so high,
Happy Valley lush lawn
South Pacific gracing the sky.

"Please help to keep it
nice, clean and tidy,"
Star Ferry to Kowloon
meet you at Central, noon.

Holiday greeting lights
flowing, moving, changing
colors and graphics in
the Victoria harbour nights.

Kowloon central park
exotic birds on display,
pick up a trick for the day
don't get caught there at dark.

Lunching at noon by day
laughing, shopping for sales
let's leave now Causeway Bay,
hop on the busy MTRailway.

Down the busy Hennesy road
seeing Lockhart, Jaffe and
Glouchester alone as I strode
along from crossing to crossing.

Ocean Park maybe at dark
but wait, day trip to Stanley
beach or Repulse Bay for
the day and shop or eat at WOK.

Let's make plans to go to
the north, Big Wave Bay,
oh that's right you're so busy
or sick, blow me off this way.

Hey let's scarf some Vietnamese
for breakfast lunch and dinner,
spring rolls and noodle soup
fancy or not, yes if you please.

Let's have some Sushi
for the price of a small country,
no let's just hang at a place
J J's, you lose great face.

Up in the morning Victoria park
geez man am I actually out here
at 4 am with the cotton tops
doing Tai Chi Chuan in the dark?

Mainland China sounds good
the pattern set by you
the question is if you should.
Blowoff blowoff this is
typical, I knew you would.

I think I know how to
travel to Guangzhou,
sit next to the nicest man
Chan, the ping pong man.

Very old political hotel once
under strict communist rule,
floor monitors, stinky sheets,
funny looks to me, I won't tell.

The souvie in hand
absolutely would have

to be the visa stamp from
the Republic of China man.

THE FAIR

The "frisbee" located over there
oh look a winter Hong Kong fair.
Oh come on let's go for fun there
nothing like the wind frantically
ripping through our hair.

I see a tear drop there,
are you okay?
This is a love affair
you really do care.

You were brave enough to go
with me to the Kowloon fair
it's late many people riding scary
rides in the cool winter air.

Seeing you at a glance
wind caressing your hair
I love you, do you know
how much I really care.

MR. NAUGHTY

Your interest and care
for little children
reminds me of angels
descending from heaven.

You are so special, caring
and wonderful when I see
you discussing what the
kids are taught and learning.

Their little brains learn, learn
as they consume info and burn.
You are as delicious as a peach
because you love to teach.

You love passing on your
infinite education and knowledge,
I hope you inspire others to do
as well as you did in college.

You're to me so beautiful
and ever present and dutiful.
I am your student full of rush,
no wonder Mr. Naughty has a crush.

When a child is acting bad
oh how the parents are sad.
When a child is not so good
subsequently to Mr., they're naughty.

Stories of catching whales,
stories of swimming with
real sharks from above
like a suspended snail.

"Are you kidding me?
Oh no Mr. Naughty,
this is a story of two
lovers diving in the sea."

PEAK PERFORMANCE

Oh how romantic
a perfectly dark corner,
the two of us are bound
together forever, now,
looked at as one loner.

Hey skippy where's my wine?
I stop to consider my
presentation, whaddya think?
Yeah now's the perfect time.

I bathe you with charm, cherish,
praise you for your strength,
I went back on my word about
a promise here comes an
unexpected mind blowing speech.

Spit it out get to the point
oh this is hard it's of some length.
You deserve this you've been great
isn't this the beautiful perfect date.

Surprise look at the size
of your beautiful brown eyes,
the birth of the Titanic
your response is "gigantic."

95

I watch you admiring something
of beauty and opulence from afar,
you are overwhelmed in love I hope
you know how special you are.

This has never been done to
you it's a beautiful score,
I'll cherish your reaction
the moments before.

Tram tram this isn't a scam
my dear if you haven't discovered
as of yet in our being together
I'm a romantic that's how I am.

Always remember there's more
for you that cometh from this spring,
oh how beautiful on your finger it
looks like your first lovers ring.

Ching ching yeah it cost
but remember this, nothing
could come close to your
love if I suffered this loss.
Your peak performance.

THE YEAR

Oh dear "1" has come and passed
this could be serious let's enjoy
the time the laughter and love,
don't be foolish in taking a pass.

I'm waiting, I'm waiting.
My dear we have a gift
we've been blessed
from the heavens above.

I wait for your decision
just don't hesitate on continuing
our destiny my love, the two of us
received the rare gift from
the blessed heavens above.

It's true we're to be together
as birds of the same feather,
my love we were meant
to always flock together.

My love, my love come to me
come to me I want to understand
about the two of us as lovers
to be together is our destiny.

Pineing, pineing yes I'm whining
my dear love don't discount our
destiny oh sweet love all you have
to do is come be with me.

Yes we had a fight you were aloof.
When friends travel as I have half
way around the world it's terrible
to treat the other as a spoof.

You tell me you need time
to make a decision of our
future together, but yet
you dangle in front of me
and taunt the easy thought.

You know what you should do
we've been through much, this is true.
The only reason you can't
make up your confused mind
parents blackmailing you, stay behind.

All the hardcore romance
and love making was our
year long undertaking,
you treat it as dirty feet
to wash away at the
end of your silly day.

THE NIGHT OF THE LAST

As we lay horizontal before a space
we are together in a far off place.
Flashing, sparkling, glimmering lights
changing shapes in the night.

Mountain tops consumed by
the clouds of condensation,
man made structures big and tall
cascading like an uneven wall.

Exception of the interior light
is that cast through God's night?
Gazing deep into the windows
of your soul my eyes are transfixed
clammering to your deepest thoughts.

Nary a word, nary a blink we let
that magical moment transport us
for hours to a location for lovers
whom are truly whole.

Silhouettes in strange shapes
cover your face as though it
were a veil tempting
me to peak within the hole.

Little did we know that magic
carpet upon which we rode
would take us to a place
only a few lucky go.

I share this moment in
words with others but
only you my true love
can really know.

Suffice it to say not long
after I cry alone, then I go.
Only you my one true love
understand and know.

Standing in a suit of birth
staring out through the space
of images wondering where
this love will go.

A tear forms in my eye
heart starting to pound
and slowly break as I turn
towards you, I already know.

FLIGHT OF NIGHT

I cry, I cry I'm so sullen
cramped and isolated.
Dim are the cabin lights
the long long flight of night.

Sigur Ros' with Icelandic boots
tears of fears I'm loosing you.
I cry, I cry my aching heart
wouldn't care if this machine
in mid-air fell apart.

Eerie sounds of Icelandic roots
is this heaven or hope.
I have to live, I want to live
so that to you my love I
may completely give.

Turnout the lights
and finish crying this.
Again I will return on
this flight of the night.

5 A. History of WINTER, AGAIN

November had come and we had been apart now for 4 months. It was complete torture for the two of us. This time apart had been so hard for us. Of course she hadn't dealt with the horrific experiences I had to endure. She only dealt with relocating to be with her family.

We both had to make major adjustments in our lives, but the most exciting thought in my mind on the way to the airport was we would soon be together and all bad things would be forgiven and we would make passionate love for a solid month. I tried not to focus on the latest revelations she informed of concerning her past scandal, but two factors were still prevelant: she had told me a huge lie and the little troll attorney asked me to give him a beating. He deserved to utilize his hospitalization insurance. He must have recently renewed it.

My dilemas in the previous months not only included the WTC attacks, but my place of employment was directly affected, I threw my ghetto roommate out of my apartment because she and her cats were disgusting and she was scamming on her portion of the bills to be paid. And finally my love had left me. Tough time.

All I could think of was my sweet young love. Love does conquer all or at least the illusion of being in love allows one to be more resilient to pain and anguish. We were together, but we were apart. One image stuck in my mind during the countdown to getting on the plane and that was the two of us embracing tightly.

I was excited at the thought of seeing my lover, but deep down I wondered how our first sight of one another would be. Could we pick up where we left off. The feelings of past resurrected or not?

I read, I slept, I watched the in-flight movies and I ate. That's what she told me to do. She advised me not fight the time while in flight and enjoy what I could because it was a long flight. She told me to hide my time pieces because there was no sense in checking the time frequently.

So I took her advise and flowed with the nature of my flight. I swear it was a test of my patience, but the means was justified by the ends. I saw two sunrises and almost two sunsets. The flight status map kept me informed of the progress realizing soon I would be there.

When I got close to H.K. I could see lights and some islands and a part of the world I was only familiar with through the media. The view was fascinating as we descended down through the clouds coming closer to touching down on a runway in S. E. Asia, Hong Kong.

I was excited at the fact of getting off that damn airplane after 24 hours of flying. I was more excited at the spectacular views of the surrounding mountains nestled on small islands in the sea of China. I saw lights and activity on the ground just before touching down.

I felt different already before stepping off of the plane because of the entire situation leading up to that very moment. The new faces and new culture made my eyes as big as golf balls and I was eating it up. While I wandered through customs and the airport looking for my love I kept thinking what will be her first reaction when we see each other for the first time in 4 months.

After a cold and eerie greeting from her at the airport I was on my way to Times Square, downtown Hong Kong. When we first saw each other in the airport, rather than showing affection, her cold reception as told through her eyes made me wonder if I had made a mistake. It was not a comfortable feeling she gave me in the beginning.

I was tired from flying, but also energized about seeing her. She made me schlep through the subway system like a slave dragging my bags and whatever reserves of energy I had were burnt at that point. Still I turned a blind eye to negative feelings because after all this trip was to be fun and regardless of her actions I was going to enjoy my venture. I am that secure. I believe in the "happy-go-lucky" school of thought.

After a back breaking experience getting to my hotel I took in the view of Hong Kong from my room. I was elated to see things I had never seen before. I immediately jumped her bones for a couple of hours to relieve my pent up fluids. Oh baby, that was what I needed.

We went for a cocktail and we gazed into each others eyes while we talked and caught up on the time past. She told me of her new endeavors and I told her I loved her. She told me of her new found excitement of returning home and I told her I loved her. I told her of the terrible experience of the WTC's and she didn't respond.

We went back to my hotel and I jumped her bones for couple of more hours. I asked her to spend the night and she reacted strangely stating she had to go home. I informed her that she was a big girl now and she didn't have to honor the parental curfew, but she gave off some weird vibes as though she was afraid of me being there in H.K.. Regardless, I still planned on having a good time discovering new discoveries.

I could hardly control my energy the first few days I was in H.K.. I had the worst case of jet lag. Took me eight days to recover because when I should have been sleeping, east coast time, I was awake. When I was awake I should have been sleeping. I would wake at 3 & 4 a.m. H.K. time. I would sleep at 3 & 4 p.m. H.K. time. This is an understatement about disorientation.

Hong Kong was fascinating. She and I made plans to do everything that H.K. had to offer. I had a month to experience as many new things as I desired. I specifically wanted to observe the people while trudging through their daily routines and rituals of living life.

I wanted to see the artsy nightlife, eat at great restaurants and see magnificent landscapes. I wanted to do so many things and I didn't know where to start and I was hungry that first morning. So I started with a traditonal H.K. buffet breakfast in the hotel restaurant. Dim Sum for breakfast is actually very good.

It took days for me to believe I was actually in H.K.. I went to parks, museums, street fairs and anything that captured my attention and imagination. When walking through the streets I didn't have any destination or least I wouldn't head directly to a location. I banged around the small streets and out of the way places. Of course I was in the downtown mixes many times too.

She let me down on many ocassions by blowing me off when we were going to get together, but there were other times she delivered. There was an eeriness about her that told me she had something to say. So as we planned to go to mainland China, I ended up going by myself because once again she blew me off.

Hong Kong truly is beautiful and all that it offers in the sense of exotic hedonism. And the women are so beautiful.

The harbour view from either Kowloon or H.K. is absolutely magnificent. One day while I crossed the harbour on the ferry I noticed a ferriswheel off in the distance. It was a damn H.K. fair. I wanted to blow my mind so I talked her into going with me one night. It was like pulling teeth because she was feeling lazy.

We struggled to get there by cab after crossing the harbour. The cab driver didn't know where the fair was. So she translated for me, "it's that way." The freaking fair was so big I became confused as to how a cabby wouldn't know such an event is taking place right on the harbour.

105

We had the best time playing games and riding rides. I talked her into going on this one ride. Certainly it didn't look as scary from the ground, but of course once you get in the saddle it's a different story. This ride had the longest line of any rides.

She started the venture brave and excited. So did I. After we boarded the ride and the disc started in motion I didn't know if she would hang in there. This disc went high and fast, swung like a pendulum, rotated like a flying saucer and scared her to death. The ride was not that scary, but it sure made scrambled eggs of your intestines.

I glanced over at her next to me and she started tearing from one eye. I shouted, "Are you okay?" She had trouble speaking because she was on the verge of spewing dinner all over the other riders, including me. I told her to look the other way. She hung in there despite the color of her face. When she got off the ride I noticed she had "sea legs." The ground was a little wobbly. I took a photo of her just after disembarkation. She tried to be flattering.

She worked teaching children english at a school. She enjoyed passing on her knowledge. She was very bright, sometimes. She had the kids eating out of her hands because she was younger than the other educators. I certainly got the impression she enjoyed being around children. She wasn't that much older than her students.

The stories she told of the students were cute. I asked her if any one student really adored her or had a crush on her. She started to tell me about this one particular boy. She described him as shy, quiet, well mannered and neatly dressed.

One day this boy told her about naughty people. He explained some people that don't do what they were supposed to do were considered naughty. She got the biggest kick out of his vocabulary and the sincerity in his eyes when he said, "naughty." I asked her if I would be considered naughty because of my activities. She responded by saying, "you should be locked up for your naughty ways."

Mr. Naughty was a daily topic for us. She imitated him in such an adorable way I wanted to meet him. She never arranged that. She told me of another story when he went fishing with his pop. He was serious when he told about the whale his father caught.

She told him of her diving experience in the Keys swimming with a shark. He couldn't believe she would swim with sharks. She tried to convince him, but he couldn't accept the fact a girl swam with a shark. He said, "that's a boys job."

The month of my visit seemed to drag at times, but then it also flew right by. I had only a couple of days left before departing for home. She and I enjoyed a lot of activities together during my visit. We should have experienced much more if it weren't for the arrogance she displayed sometimes.

However, I wanted to do something very special for her before I left. Despite our disagreements and fighting because of her attitude I still loved her and planned the most romantic and eventful evening for us at a place located on the top of the tallest mountain in H.K.. This dynamic place over looks the rest of H.K.. It's the most spectacular view I've ever seen.

We arrive at the establishment and everything between us is fine. She has no idea of what I am going to do to her heart that evening. It was all good. I picked a table furthest from other tables. We had the most spectacular view of H.K. I was hungry and anxious.

I wanted her to know how much I appreciated her and how much I missed her while we were apart. In the past I joked with her about marriage and the main thrust of this trip was not about marriage. Still I love giving gifts and watching people's reaction. I already gave to her gifts when I first arrived in H.K..

I have exquisite taste and go first class never compromising quality. I told her a story and then presented her with a fabulous gift. She was so surprised and apprehensive while opening her gift. I told her not to worry about me proposing marriage. She opened her gift and almost had a heart attack. She actually was lost in searching for words. I stumped her mind.

She told me no matter what she would never part with this gift. She loved it so much I caught her admiring her new acquisition many times throughout the night. It was a beautiful sight on her hand and she knew it. She told me I was spoiling her and I informed her that was my intention.

We had been together already for a year. I really cared for this young woman and at times she cared for me. She kept trying to bait me with her indecision of whether or not we should stay together. We talked about the pros and cons of our relationship.

We had an argument in which we didn't speak for a few days because of her aloofness one evening when we were out. She was rude and inconsiderate and shined me on. I didn't like it so I told her to remember I traveled halfway around the world to see and be with her.

So, her attitude was showing her ungratefulness for my troubles in coming to see her. I would have treated her like family if the shoe were on the other foot. It's unpleasant when you treat someone as a stranger when they traveled a long distance to be with that person.

She told me she didn't have 100% confidence in our relationship, but not because of me. This statement was based on her selfdoubts. She kept crying out the word "options." There's no room in a relationship for options when the hearts come into play. Options are available when you buy a car or order from a restaurant menu.

She kept telling me she would make a decision after I left H.K.. I urged her to be brave and deal with the decision face to face like adults and not to show cowardice by doing it behind my back. We were close and this communication was the basis of our relationship, being able to talk to one another.

Her big decision made me feel like a gameshow contestant. Would I win the big prize or be sent away with a parting gift. Not fare and I refused to deal with it on that level. I gave her my best voice of reason.

She knew before I arrived in H.K. what her decision was. I saw it in her eyes at the airport. I prepared for the worst and hoped for the best. I tried to convince her to be brave about it. She was a puppet on a string for the sake of "options." So shallow.

Our last night together was spent in my hotel room. She arrived late because of some worthless excuse. I was busy packing and my mind set dealt with already being home. When she arrived she had her agenda written all over face.

The last romantic evening we would spend together until we would meet again was so delightful and sexy. I turned out all of the lights and opened my curtains to reveal a H.K. skyline. The huge windows exposed us to the mountains tops of the H.K. skyline graced by low lying clouds of condensation.

We made love numerous times that evening and poored every little bit of passion we had in our bodies and hearts into our last night. It was sad and beautiful at the same moment. Still we realized after being removed from one another for a period of time we still loved making love to one another. She was so lushious and I lapped up every little last drop of her I could.

She couldn't make love anymore and pushed me away so that she could regain her breath. We both went breathless at that point. We lay on the bed naked and soiled from making wild passionate love only to stare into each others eyes. We didn't say one word for an hour. We caressed each other and kissed and gazed deep into each others soul.

The silence between us was golden as everything that needed to be said had already been said many times before. We were transported to a mystical and spiritual place in life. I loved this girl more than any other that I can remember. My traveling there proved it by her own admission.

I got up from the bed naked and stood at the large window gazing out over the magnificent mountainous skyline. I couldn't take the pain of knowing we weren't going to remain together after this last night. She asked me what was the matter and I turned to her and said, "oh nothing my love."

We made the plan for her come to the hotel that morning of my departure and see me off. Reciprocal gesture like when she moved back to H.K.. I saw her off to the airport. The only problem is she called me when she got home that night and backed out of the plan.

I was really disappointed in her. Again, she came up with some transparent excuse. I let her off the hook and said, "it's okay." Really I was upset at her nerve of dangling again another aspect of our relationship in my face only to be teased with the outcome. That was very cold and calculating and only a child wouldn't understand that.

I was late for the flight, but not by my fault. On the way to the airport I felt alone because the night just past conceivably was the last time we might see each other. I knew she didn't want to continue seeing me. It was too difficult for her. But there again she had no backbone or bravado.

I was sweating profusly by the time I boarded the airplane because I had to run a certain stretch through the airport. A security official made me open my bag looking for a weapon. It was only a pair of nail clippers. I found them and told the security personnel, "it's yours, a gift."

The flight was full unlike the flight going to H.K.. What a drag because I wouldn't be able to stretch out and sleep. I felt this was going to be a long flight. Thank god I had a good book to read. In between watching movies, sleeping, eating, and reading I listened to the airplane music and found this most amazing channel.

The songs I heard on this channel from one particular group was truly amazing in that I had never heard such sounds before. My heart was already weak and sad and these songs were so melancholy maybe this combination is what grabbed my attention. At one point I turned the overhead light out and cried while listening to these songs. They were eerie and beautifully captured my state of mind at that particular time.

Kent Abbett

<u>RETURN OF DISCONTENT</u>

YOU ARE EVERYWHERE

I see you here and see you there
walking, sitting in the park
daylight hours even in the dark,
your face is all over the place.

Little leaves blowing across
the field, I see you moving
along the sacred ground
like angels soaring through
the heavens gate.

People here, people there
tall, short, people of your
culture you're everywhere.
My thoughts of you, I care.

Love is an involuntary
reflex of the senses,
held deep inside not
always accessible
except when accentuated.

I see your ying to my yang
golden lotus accepting stalk
of jade, like clouds making
love with the heavens rain.

I see your heavenly flower
blossoming with it's hedy
scent encompassing my
encouragement of pillow book.

Hard is the way the mind
and heart works like beehives
producing golden honey
thick and rich with essential
nutrients to feed the hunger.

A faithful heart makes wishes,
for those brave enough to
labor with their soul's mind,
come true for me and you.

<u>YOUR EYES</u>

The photo of you at two
your beautiful animated
passionate eyes in my hand
photo's of you now,
not one but two.

No longer are you two,
the fledgling woman
you are at twenty–two,
oh how I love you.

I've seen these eyes before
when two were in the
throws of passion still
when it was the break
of the new day, four.

I've seen these eyes before
now that oceans separate
the two of us I feel you
have started to look for
the proverbial door.

Not fare, so hair will grow
here there everywhere

because a lover's heart
should never endure
this pain, it's not fare.

Nasal hair, cranium hair,
nary to shave a hair
shall grow it everywhere,
not to trim a single hair
until our love is deemed fare.

HAPPY NEW YEAR, TOO

Oh my the dreaded call
you made the fateful
day of the new year,
my mind hit
the proverbial wall.

Pain pain oh please away,
oh pain why are you today.
I'm sick not from the call
but oh hell all things combined
made my heart fall.

Your timing is terrible
with this being your
final decision I might
write a parable.

I can't believe what I'm
hearing, this to John from
Jane, why not face to face
this is a cowards place.

Yeah, yeah happy new
year to youse too,
should have my head
examined to see why
I still do love you.

CHARM, CHARM

If I'm good I can charm
her right back into my arm
and be done with the pain,
anguish, heartache and harm.

Because you've chosen
to remain beside me, my friend,
it's like being stung a
thousand times by bees.

The fire in a swarm
the heartache
like a rustic, tragic barn
on a beautiful old farm.

I must muster up an extra
romantic dose of charm
to have you swoon and
collapse into my arm,
the antecdote for harm.

SUFFER, SUFFER

The other side of the
world is a cruel buffer,
I can't see or touch you
through the many hills
and layers of clouds.

I worry for your happiness
I worry for your heart,
is it as much torture for
you as it is for I,
if only I could fly.

Like birds of winter to be,
when you are a mere
passing thought to me
I drop to one knee.

When I cry out your
name you can't hear me
because my hand is blocking
the throat like a muffler
why do I have to suffer.

TROUBLE MAKER

I pressured your mind,
you become a boilermaker
as a result of your hastiness,
do you consider me a trouble maker?

I'm not a simple quaker or a
fancy bread baker just a regular
guy wanting to shower you with
unprecedented love, are these
words of a trouble maker?

I wined you, I dined you
told you great stories from
the past and then you smiled
hugged me and laughed.

I couldn't help but think
because of our love for
one another this beautiful
romance would forever last,
am I a infinite trouble maker?

IS IT ABOUT YOU OR ME

Why can't the decision be we,
I made the romance about yours and you,
but because of your selfish ways
to me you decided to put the screw.

I gave more than enough
credit for which you weren't due,
did I make the fatal mistake
of forgetting me, make too much you?

We carried on laughing, running
smiling all the day especially Sunday,
all I ever wanted from you was to
sometimes make US about me.

Your lack of compassion is
inconsiderate and childish,
the only reason in mind
this was your ultimate wish,
you flounder like a worthless fish.

Your speeches of options
consequently have become
your fatal "floptions,"
humans are not available on
menus or price lists of cars.

123

Options when dealing with
the heart show lack of soul
and not creative art within
your head, your soul is dead,
enjoy your "floptions."

YES, YES LET'S TALK

Despite your character flaws,
if we talk I can keep you
in the throngs of my mind,
no this is torture, I'm sad
I'm upset with you.

What I want, what I want
you know what I want.
I'm angry with your
aloofness, we should talk.

This period of silence
between us is the hardest
decision ever I've had to
undertake, I'm tormented,
sad and drifting off into space.

Silence is golden,
my anxiety from
this awful situation
is making me an olden.

Oh how I wish this
situation we would squish,
taking a long wooden
handle to a garbage fish.

125

Kent Abbett

How sorry I am, I may
have upset you.
After you corrected me
I became humbled like
a little lamb, how sorry I am.

MOVING AT DIFFERENT SPEEDS

You and me are traveling
together at different speeds.
The numeric value differential
can you speed up?

You want me to slow
down, oh no have to read
the road signs ahead
this is your driving lesson.

Oh man now what,
dangerous curves,
what's next ahead
the road starts to swerve.

Divided highway begins,
ends now it's time to yield.
Where's my protection
shield against the field.

Merge, merge don't we
feel the important urge,
the only sign I'm looking
for with you is LOVE.

127

STRIKE OUT BE BOLD

Risk risk, tsk tsk now
is the time in your life
to not be risk averse,
be bold before you get old.

The regret you'll have
is the "what if" reflection
when you've grown old
and your heart is cold.

Support I proposed for
you, consider it like mold
strike out now on your
own, be brave be bold.

Let's play house because
I showed you, pushed you
tried to teach you what
is self reliance ultimately.

The strings controlling you
are like that of a puppet, far
be it from me to make you dangle
there are two other familiar people
that have put you in this tangle.

In order for two lovers
to reunite you must strike
out and be bold before
you know it you'll get old.

Hence trust in what
I say today because
I know what you don't
know, it's independence.

SHARING

Sharing is the ultimate
caring my loved one.
Food on your plate
taxi for a date.

Events of your day
the bed you sleep in.
These are struggles
that with another you slay.

Caring is really sharing
my young loved one.
Feeding me grapes,
traveling together like
birds of the same feather.

Sharing, sharing my senses
are off I seem to be less caring.
Input of information is falling off,
feelings are now not forthright.

Are you absolutely
sharing your true feelings?
Like the skin of fruits,
disposable are the feelings
hence the fruits peelings.

No longer the sense,
feelings are wearing
less and less is your sharing
hence you have no longer caring.

Oh my dear love this does
mean there's no more caring,
the truth of your feelings
are the proof of the dealings.

Oh be true, do be true
if I sense no longer the
sharing oh my dear love
it will break my heart.

I now know we are threw
sharing has to be true,
between us otherwise
there is no me and you.

HINGED

Looking, looking
I'm hungry now
I start cooking,
tired of looking.

Eagerly anticipating
sounds and words
from you, check the
lines again soon my
life must begin.

Every few minutes
my maniacal behavior
recycles again, oh
what a syndrome
when does life begin.

The health of dashing
back and forth, wishing
and hoping words from
you only hinders the
daily ritualistic actions.

My mind ponders what
was your day like, I only

wish I was listening to your
melancoly voice and words.

I'm hinged and flapping
like an old wooden shutter
in the wind waiting, anticipating
why aren't you willing to
engage in our telecommunication.

ACT OF DESERTION

Every so often there was curl
if I'd listened to my intuition then
rather than now I'd have known
you were an ungrateful little girl.

So let it be said
forever may these
words of wisdom
stay in your head.

I tried, you lied
I gave you made
me into your
pitiful slave.

And again I tried
with your vicious
intentions again
you made me cry.

Half a world away
as I sit and write today,
if we ever cross
paths again it will
not be about again.

For me never again
will I be the one
to take it on the chin,
so let the oh so painful
healing for me begin.

The whole in your soul
will never be filled again,
because of your inferiority
complex and low self
esteem we won't ever
be able to build a team.

Watching the sky for stars
thought I'd found the
brightest by far,
but it fizzled and drizzled.

So, so long through
this bitter sweet swan song,
I am long gone from
pain and heartache never
a great love will you make.

What will become months
from now 2,4,6,
or more, if only I felt like
keeping an honest score of
what we feel then, not again.

135

SECRETS TO BE TOLD

Hush hush sweet darling
for the secrets I behold,
for you the duty in strict confidence
never to reveal to the source,
you must be told.

I once had a beautiful friend
my closest friend,
a friend of trust,
a confidential friend,
my friend of lust.

My friend was everything, student,
teacher, lover, confidant, sister,
therapist, mother, angel and
goddess of the heavens.
I truly miss my friend.

My best friend went away
maybe to never return someday.
I long lonely for my best friend
to return regardless of the inevitable.

I desire my friend, my buddy,
my pal, my animal lover, to return

to me and continue the old way.
The animal misses his animal friend.

Suffice it to say the return of the day
will never come my very best friend,
ninja animal, doesn't understand
how to succumb.

So my friend I tell you this
as a deep secret for you to behold,
if you cross paths with my once
best friend I trust that she can't be told.

THE REAL YOU...P.U.!

Are you set then bounce this,
I'm only going to tell you
what you need to know,
then on cue you can go.

Need attention get a therapist
to help you with your lisp.
You trip over your own ankles
but this trip will forever change
your limp.

Heard your metamorphic
cries girl to woman.
Showed you the way
comforts of staying a girl suit you,
the wrong side of the fence.

Tell me if your heart's in this
my saving grace now leaves
you alone, lonely, standing
by yourself in recycled lace.

Your bovine scathology is where
you will always exist,
floundering, flopping like a pig
trying to unearth the twig.

The loss of a lover and great friend
seems to be your m.o. and trend,
how can a schemer and scamer
expect to succeed at this trend,
my young idiotic friend?

The ice coarsing through
your veins is vane.
Your time wasted is slime tasted,
the board of health
should be notified.

The problem for a man falling
in love with a tramp is,
when cerebellum is of a child.
A child not wild not mild,
but just a child that's stupid.

Your lying, cheating and deceiving
is how to get ahead in life,
but in the end your many sores
will keep you in score.

Smooth like sandpaper
disposer of the human race,
from whence you came?
Man did you ever lose face.

Ce' la vie

139

6 A. History of RETURN OF DISCONTENT

After a few days of suffering jet lag from the return trip I bundled up and went shopping and bopping around to enjoy the nice wintery day. While bopping around I was in a daze practically stumbling on my own thoughts of her. She was the only thing in my mind. Of course my trip entirely was still deeply etched in my thoughts, but I couldn't get her face out of my mind.

I began to hallucinate every time a saw a woman of her type. I thought it was her. Then I began to imagine she was standing where ever my eyes focused. I realized that day I would never see her again and this made me sad. I wanted her and she was in my every breath.

We had come so far and reached a plateau few people spiritually can find throughout their lives. I was feeling very spiritual after my return and my emotions were not of my own thinking. I felt as though she had some sort of mystical ninja power and I was cursed by it.

I mentioned this to a friend of mine and he told me don't worry about it. He advised me to snap out of the trance I was in.

I must have had a dozen rolls of film to develop from my trip. When all the photos were developed I particularly noticed one that stunned me. It was our last night together and I took some beautiful photos of her laying on the bed after we made love. She had this rosy tint to her face as though she just had...you know.

Her eyes were magical in the photo. I remembered a photo she gave me of herself when she was 2 years old. Alas, I compared the two photos and the expression of her eyes in both photos were identical. Blew my mind.

My mind was blown for other reasons such as I didn't know what was going on between us. We hadn't spoken for several days not because of a fight, but rather her big decision took time. Mind you the problem was not geometrical or physics in nature. Simple decision.

I was feeling down and hurt. A smathering of self pity just to season me for the season. The early winter blues. I donned heavy clothes and overgrown hair to fight off the winter blues.

Somehow I acquired food poisoning on New Year's Eve. I certainly ate something that didn't agree with me. The holiday cheer didn't taste great coming back up either. I was sick and in bad shape. I saw the New Year come in with my head stuck in the commode.

The next morning I woke up feeling like death warmed over. I was not my usual self when the day began because of my immediate problem and my heart was ill. I hadn't heard from her now for two weeks. I dropped an e-mail a couple of days previous but no response. Whatever.

The phone rang. It was her. She called to wish me a Happy New Year and to breakup with me. I told her there was much to do about her timing and diplomacy. Her response was, "my heart's not in it anymore." That's convenient.

I asked her where had she been. We hadn't spoken in a couple of weeks. Her excuse was, "I was taking my time trying to decide." I was crushed at that very moment. I had prepared myself for this time, but one can never really prepare. Besides I had to go regurgitate.

When asked why didn't she break her decision to me when I saw her, something fare, she started babbling off reasons for us not being together. The excuses were contrived and rehearsed. Whatever.

We agreed to remain friends and keep in touch with one another. It was one of the hardest conversations I had ever had to discuss. I started getting choked up and had to excuse myself. I was racked as though I had been on a drinking binge and that's okay if the pursuit was fun at least. I was not having fun. I passed out the rest of the day.

I had often joked about my relationship with her was so magical it would be great in a story. I really believed that. What a great romantic story. One day when I was jogging the sudden thought ocurred to me how I could get her back in my arms. Write a beautiful story about our relationship. What better to "woo" a woman with than poetry.

My body and mind were in a state of flux and I was out of control. I sat and started writing what was in my head. That's to say she was in my head. This was tough and I didn't know any other way to deal with my immediate emotions other than to create something expressing how I felt.

When we would speak I would tell her of my newest writing project. She chuckled. I was amazed at her disbelief in my abilities. But I had already written some 3 dozen poems and I was far from finished.

I tried to keep busy with things. Trivial they may have been, but I needed to get my mind off of her and us. Time to move on. Easier said than done. My suffering was relentless and the only way to stave off my pain was to get lost in something new. I once was lost in her and now I needed my new direction.

We were communicating frequently with one another and this wasn't helping either one of us. It was proving to make matters more difficult.

I was ready to go back to reclaim her love as mine, but she shot down the idea.

I wanted her to be happy and her endeavors interested me, just so long as it wasn't with another man. I knew her elation was hidden in our conversations. I sensed she needed to be with someone locally. Of course she was a needy attention getter anyhow.

Everytime I thought of her I became weak. This trend was happening every other minute. I reached a point of not functioning. She confided in me she couldn't sleep at nights. We both had reached a state of mild depression. Still I couldn't understand why she invited such pain, again, for the two of us.

During our conversations she confessed her uncertainty about her decision. Her fickle contradictions were driving me crazy. I reminded her to "stop floundering for the halibut." I was pushing her to give substance to her decision making process. Decide one way or the other and let me know, but stop torturing me with the petty rituals.

We were still in love with one another and we found it hard to break away from the year of love. It was so confusing what was going on. Of course I wasn't letting go of her that easy. I was fighting for her love and I was losing the contest. I am not a good loser.

More and more of our conversations seemed to be focused always on her. I finally reminded her that there was two of us in the romance. It was a suttle hint to her I was tired of being drained by her and all of her terrible woes. And what, I 'm chopped liver.

I left myself unprotected in the relationship and now it was time for me to concentrate on me for a change. I was not having fun with her in my life any further. I kept reminding her to stop being selfish and be compassionate towards my feelings for a change. It would have been nice every so often if we discussed me.

I asked her if my love wasn't good enough for her. She blathered about keeping her options open. I asked, "what options?" She had some scheme about her options and how they fit into the world according to the E generation philosophy. I explained to her all generations have a mission, but they all end up at the same cross roads and this is what life was about. Real life is in the daily rituals not in some music video.

She became caluous towards me and that was okay because she didn't understand what I knew about life, obviously, but to coach her on what life was about she didn't need help because she had already figured this out.

She wanted to pursue something in the arts, but yet the easy way out of struggling in life for her was to go the corporate route. She fantasized about being a corporate slug. I told her, that life stymied the creative process in human beings and lack of imagination was the reason most corporate jockeys walk around in a rut.

She was confessing to me she had lost her soul sometime since returning home. That was depressing because she had no idea how boring she would become. I don't mean she would be bored, but that she would become a boring person and it was already obvious in her conversations.

She was upset at some of our conversations we had recently so we didn't speak for a small period of time. Actually she was being a spoiled brat like she wanted to be. So I let her.

The cut off from communication was torture because we hadn't really had a chance to discuss some unresolved issues. Her attitude was "I don't want to talk about it." I did want to talk about the terrible mean things she had done to me and the awful way she had treated me towards the end of our romance. I needed to air-it-out.

She refused to deal with my emotions and feelings in the lurch she had left me in. The least she could do was listen and be a friend, but that was not an option. We had a minor blow out between us. Again it had to do with her ca-ca attitude.

I lectured her on a few facts of life. She didn't like being lectured as most people don't, but when a fool starts to screw up people around them an intervention moment is necessary. She flipped at my remark about me making a mistake by loving such a young girl. She asked me, "are you sure you should be telling me this?" I remembered not stuttering. What a shame when outsiders have to provide guidance that parents don't.

I was trying to get over the heartache and she was not helping me through the hard time. I didn't like her stoic interest in what I had to say. So I said what I could in a short breath and we screamed at each other and hung up the phone.

The sad reality had set in we weren't meant to be together at this time or so she thought. She was just getting started with her life and I was already in the race of life. I travel at mach-three with my hair on fire.

Living loose and carefree was comfortable for me. I'm not conservative.

I told her I wished she were further along in her life so that we weren't disrupted right in the middle of something great. She kept copping the plea of being to young to be committed to a love. Well that was cool with me if it were true, but I knew there was someone whispering in her ears not to follow her heart. The voice said, "do what I tell you even though it goes against your real wishes."

I knew how to drive and how to negotiate road hazards. She didn't drive and she couldn't negotiate road hazards. Each road bump I explained to her was an obstacle in life. This was okay because you learn how to negotiate obstacles. She wasn't a good negotiator, trust me.

We agreed no one was to blame for the unfortunate timing of our falling in love, although the flipside of her proclaimation about wrong timing was not my belief. I believed we could be together. My car went faster than hers. Her car wasn't even started. I tried to encourage her to get out there and jump in the race. She wanted to control the race, but that is not reality.

She was watching too many "reality shows" which aren't about reality, but rather manipulating audiences into believing the world works like the show. Well of course this is a contrived and convoluted perspective of the real world and the tendencies to warp the minds of viewers is overwhelming and obvious through their behavior.

So sad when a person so desperately wants to be independent, but they are conflicted and afraid to let go of the security net. I explained to her at some point and time the big bird is going to encourage baby bird to fly away from the nest. Once a certain age is reached by an individual the parents job is done and the parents want the baby to leave.

We were speaking again and she was in a state of depression and emotional turbulence. Me being the true friend proposed something to her she had never considered because of her confused thoughts. She wanted this and that and so I asked her how did she plan on achieving these goals. She had no more of an idea than the man on the moon, whom by the way hadn't been on the moon in some decades.

I tried to give her guidance and direction. I told her to come live with me. I would support her and provide her with every basic need while she was establishing herself in the world. Besides, the industry she wanted to pursue, her corporate endeavors, was where I lived.

I emphasized to her what true independence meant and that was jumping out there into the world and experimenting with what works and what doesn't. Her big plans were no different from any other person's plans, but she didn't understand the common sense approach.

After shooting down my tempting offer she proclaimed, "I'll do it under my own terms." I provoked her to take the risk, be bold. Do what others haven't done and stop trying to be beyond her own intelligence. Build wisdom through experience not through plans on a napkin.

She couldn't quite grasp the reality of young adults her age or younger taking risks and learning from their intelligence rather than relying on what was learned in a book. In other words there's no substitute for actual life experience except MORE life experience. She was not as brave as she imagined herself to be.

She had always kept her true feelings and thoughts in her subconsciousness which meant not only was she untrue to herself, but to others very close to her. Her upbringing and culture supressed this basic human need and she had yet to overcome her setbacks. I informed her of these flaws and she became upset. Her attitude was, "who the hell are you to be telling me this." That statement alone suffices for a summation.

My enlightenment to her was some sort of bad event. I guess no person in her life had ever been brutually honest with her and this was a sad fact. I encouraged her to understand human feelings are real and shouldn't be trounced or pounced upon by freewheeling idiots.

We exchanged some rather "heated" e-mails because I felt she owed me some basic apologies, but she couldn't allow her low self-esteem to deal with that. Her mistreatment and scandalous behavior involving me was dispicable and I wanted to know from her that she was still a human. She didn't get the hint and probably never will.

I informed her my actions wouldn't be understood by her presently, but perhaps she would have enough intelligence in the future to understand what my actions were about. So I offended her and repulsed her to the best of my abilities and it worked.

I had to cutoff all communications with her for my mental health because I was suffering from her bragging about her new social exploits. I really wanted to be informed of her new club discoveries and whom she was sleeping with. Remember she was a needy person and felt more secure when she manipulated people.

Again I asked what was the basis for her breakup with me and again she found the truth too much to deal with so she spewed more convenient excuses. She felt good when she lied to people as though she had great poker face. We agreed we wouldn't talk for an unspecified period of time while she "recovered" from her pain. What pain?

Weeks had passed and we had no communication between us. This was so hard because we both were addicted to the others love. It was "cold turkey" from hell. Worse than cleaning up from drug consumption because matters of the heart are real unlike artificial substances.

I sent her a reconciliation card only with a small humorous message and I thought she would respond with a simple "hello." Her actions certainly confirmed my suspicions she only wanted to distance herself as much as possible from the mess she created while in the U.S..

Still I was left to deal with her residual scandal because I knew I would run across the paths of the "scumbags" I despised so intensely. I didn't feel that was my job to clean up after her. I was her lover not her personal valet waiting to wipe her "derriere" at her liking.

I found myself constantly hinged to her voice when the phone rang or wishing she was on my phone message or that she sent me an e-mail. I felt like a rubberball bouncing between these technologies until one day I realized what a rut I had put myself in. I needed to get over her a.s.a.p. so I could carry on with my own life. I was struggling really bad.

She was like a hurricane in my life. Ripping a destructive path through my world and leaving nothing behind for me to clammer to. She literally had deserted our love, left me to deal with her messes, and turned a cold shoulder toward me, the human.

What kind of person raised this kind of a evil person. The guilty parties should be slapped about the face and neck until they realize what a burden this is to the rest of society. Why should other people have to deal with certain people's misgivings. Pretty inconsiderate by my high standards. Kids definitely act the same as their parents.

I really believe she was special in the beginning and to my good fortune I discovered she was not the person she wanted to be. She was a walking contradiction as presented by the writing on the wall. She had no soul and no character in her young life as of yet. How sad this must be for a person to go through life not understanding what a disappointing life they will lead.

I promised myself I would not acknowledge her existence on the face of this earth ever again. I have an amazing gift for predicting outcomes of future events and there would be no great loss for me to deal with. I now had regained my composure and felt protected from any more pain and threats of inferior humans.

What confronted her in her future endeavors was now completely up to her to handle and deal with in an illequiped fashion. She would come to terms with her losses sometime in the future, but I wouldn't be available to listen to her crying and complaining about, "why, why, why me?"

I conceded, privately, she was special to me at one point in my life and the year long romance was great, but to her it was just a vehicle to screw with people. I once suggested to her to get a dog so she could abuse it without serious repercussions.

I missed her deeply. I missed our time together and all inclusive activities. But she will never hear these confessions from me. She'll have to be kept in the dark about how I viewed our love and my thoughts as to what a sad individual she really was. She had potential to be a great person, but chose to take the devious route in life because it was simpler than taking responsibility for one's actions.

We hadn't communicated for several months and my feeling was we would never speak again in our lifetimes. This actually suited me well because I didn't feel like mentoring a waste of time or becoming a victim to some minor league manipulation. I've always played in the big leagues not the children's leagues.

The history of the last poem is "self explanatory!"

"This is the end, the end my friend, the end."
The Doors

About the Author

The author was born and raised in Florida. His formidable teenage years were spent in the Florida Keys contributing to the family skin-diving business.

The author was bitten by the show business bug in the early eighties and subsequently has continued in the arts for twenty years. Along the way, he received a Bachelor of Arts in International Business, lived in Toronto, Ontario Canada, ended up in NYC and has had the good fortune of traveling throughout the world.

The endeavors of the author have lead to the screenplays, *The Bends, SCORE, Cater Waiter!, Reciprocity, Nocturnal Nemesis*, and *Recoup*. Other writings include this book of poetry and the novel *Save the Robot*, and *Metamorphosis*.

Printed in the United States
1050200005B/1-93